The Power Of Mantras

Application and Effect

from

Klaus Wirtz

Bodhisattva

The Power Of Mantras

Application and Effect

from

Klaus Wirtz

Bodhissattva

Imprint

The Power Of Mantras

ISBN: 978-0-244-10623-2

Author Klaus Wirtz

klauswirtz@ymail.com

Table of Contents

Foreword

Everyone who knows me knows how much I stand by my promises and how important they are to me. Before I promise anything, I check very carefully whether I can hold these too. Hence the following promise to the reader.

I promise!

I promise you that anyone who keeps disciplined by the simple clues and consistent from start to finish will be afterwards a completely different person than he was before. He will become more successful, happier, perhaps healthier, more relaxed. He will change completely and with it his environment and his reality.

It only takes 5-10 minutes daily. If there is no time on some days or you do not feel like it, you can easily move it. However, the order of the individual mantras is important because one builds on the other slowly.

What are mantras?

Mantras are a kind of prayer that, by reciting, singing, loud or quiet, or even writing in a special way, vibrates and harmonizes the soul with the energy in the universe.

Mantras are prayers that help us to get inner peace, serenity or patience.

Mantras are prayers that help us to lose things like envy, hate, dissatisfaction, sometimes even illness.

There are countless "little" mantras that help us to tackle the daily small problems of life, many "middle" mantras that can already change the reality and fulfill simple desires and the "big" mantras that change everything, make illness disappear, etc ,

Since everything always has at least two pages, it is the same with mantras.

There are also so-called negative mantras that can harm others or even cause illness and death.

I will not go into these mantras, as I have dedicated myself to the positive change in light and love.

Of course, a person inexperienced in meditation and mantras will not be able to develop their full power, especially in the "great" mantras. But an ABC student will also have his problems with the higher philosophy.

Years of meditation and countless mantras have made me who I am and what I can accomplish.

Only these experiences put me in a position to write meaningful and honest about it, to introduce others into the application, to guide and to fulfill my promise given above.

Someone who already has some experience with meditation or mantras may find the first mantras in the later chapter "Every Day a Mantra" very simple, but then he should remember his apprenticeship and his first experiences.

In this book, I will describe some examples I have experienced, as I experienced them in my reality and from my point of view. At first, I did not always understand these "mystical" experiences, but it is not important to understand everything from the start, if the results can not be denied.

Great and well-known mantras

While everyone can learn to recite or pray and most of them feel their effects, they will not be able to fully appreciate their power and apply their power to themselves or others.

Among the best known and strongest mantras is the **"Om Mani Padme Hum".**

It is used to seek healing and compassion for all and in all, in it is the power of all discourses of Buddha, all mantras and prayers should be united.

The Om stands for the body, mind and speech of the purified Buddha.

The Mani stands for his jewel, sweetheart or diamond, so for something very precious.

Padme is similar to the lotus flower that is so important in Asia, which awakens and grows in the mud, yet is of absolute purity and flawlessness.

The Hum or sometimes Hung is for the desire to develop a strong heart.

Also a very well known and strong mantra is the **Gayatrimantra**.

OM Bhur Bhuvah Svaha, act Savitur Varenyam, Bargho Devasya Dhimahi

Dhiyo Yo Nah Prachodayath.

Gayatri the name of the goddess who watches over this mantra serves as a kind of channel our prayer to the all-encompassing light (we humans like to say sun) out of which all life is created, with whose light we can be healed.

Bhur Bhuvah Svaha stands for earth, astral plane and sky.

Did Savitur for the god of pure light and its power.

Varenyam means love or worship.

Bargho Devasya Dhimani should be translated in a different order.

Dhimani means looking at, looking at, Devasya is grace, and Bargho is the healing light. So roughly: we look at the divine grace of the healing light.

Yo Nah (which enlightens or enlightens our) Dhiyo (mind) (Prachodayath).

It is meant to help us cleanse our minds and hearts so that we are ready for enlightenment.

Another mantra I would like to mention is the **Asato Ma Mantra.**

Om

Asato Ma Sad Gamaya, Tamaso Ma Jyotir Gamaya, Mrityor Ma Amritam Gamaya.

Which has roughly the meaning for "Lead me from not being to being, from darkness to light, through death to immortality.

Of course, all translations are inadequate on the true meaning and power. Through the translations, it is even possible that these mantras create a different vibration by changing the sound and thus lose much of their own power.

"OM TARE TUTARE TURE SOHA"

Tara is a female bodhisattva, someone who has voluntarily chosen the path of everlasting rebirth until all are redeemed from their sorrows and rebirths.

With her active compassion, she wants to protect us from pride, delusion, anger, wrong views, jealousy, greed, stinginess and doubt.

Another healing mantra is the **Moola Mantra**

Om Sat Chit Ananda Parabramha Purushottama Paramatma Sri Bhagavati Sametha Sri Bhagavate Namaha Hari Om Tat Sat

I bow to the Supreme Being who is Existence, Consciousness and Bliss. I bow to the Divine manifesting in human forms and in our hearts. I bow to the feminine and male aspect of the Divine.

God is the truth - the true "BEING"

Sat means truth, Chit is consciousness and Ananda bliss and joy.

It serves as a strong connection to the divine energy that created everything, that is everything, to build and strengthen, so that this power can flow and work in us.

Loka Samasta Sukhino Bhavantu

May all beings be happy in all worlds. May all beings in all worlds fare well.

Where: Loka - the world, universe,

Samasta - all, completely

Bhavantu - they like to be

Sukhino - happiness, joy, divine blessing means

A mantra for peace, which should help to be peaceful and kind always and in all situations.

May the knowledge of the true meaning, sense, and wisdom reach you.

"SO BE IT" Thank you

There are, as mentioned at the beginning, innumerable important or less important mantras, and we often use our own little mantras without knowing it or thinking about it. Who has not even thought of a human being whom he has not seen for a long time and how often we met this person in one way or another. Coincidence? Hardly likely. Through this thinking, we recited a prayer (mantra) which was answered and fulfilled. How often do we use the word "I would like this now" or "It would be nice if that happened". Often, however, we also recite incorrectly by using the words "NOT" or "NO". In the pure energy or light, I like to use the word love in this context, there are no negative words and are not perceived. This means that when we say "I do not want this to happen to me" or "I hope I'm not unlucky" or something similar, these words "not, no," are not perceived by "being" or "destiny". Thus, a positive wish turns negative, which can lead us to get exactly the opposite of what we want.

Before I get to the main part of the book, namely the change of each (if he wants to and therefore actively participate), I would like to tell you some true stories that have changed me and my life with the help of mantras.

True stories

From my perspective "bureaucratic nonsense" I came to the deportation camp on Sri Lanka. Each of these inmates stays there until his identity papers are in order and he gets himself a plane ticket to his home country. My papers were in order and I had no other legal procedure to expect. The only thing missing was the financial means to buy me a plane ticket. Help from the embassy or family, as well as friends were not expected. Thus I adjusted myself to a longer residence time. In the end it was almost 2 years. During this time, I came closer to meditation and expressed the desire for money in the meditative state.

(I thought that I could pay for the flight) After about 1-2 weeks I got a visit from the embassy, which brought me a letter from a heir apparent. In these I was told that I had an inheritance, (as well as my three siblings) made. The testator, a maternal relative, was completely unknown to me, and I first learned of his existence with this letter.

At any rate, I thought that with this inheritance the problem of deportation camp was done. A mistake, because a brother of mine was not findable and so the inheritance did not come to the disbursement.

The meaning of the whole and why I was in the camp, I recognized later. The desire for money was fulfilled, but not the expectation that I connected with it.

Please Reflect on meaning and expectation in later wishes.

Another event was the following. Suleiman (a Pakistan born Malediwe) and I sat in the large yard outside our barracks. Here I should mention that there was a barrack for the male inmates and another barrack for the female persons. The women's tin barrack had a blue color. Suleiman and I talked about faith and spiritual things. I mentioned the change of reality and wish fulfillment in certain masses and under certain conditions was possible. He asked how. In order to have the certainty of fulfillment and to express a wish that was actually impossible in our thinking, I said "Let's change the color of the women's barrack", but he does not expect that she would be different the next day. We agreed on green. (I would like to mention here that the local police or immigration does not provide any money for such things as paint or personal belongings, even medications or medical help was only available with own funds.) So I explained that to us In our thinking for a few minutes to express the wish that the barracks would turn green. The conclusion of the mantra or prayer should be a "So be it, thank you". We implemented this. A few weeks later, a major inspection was announced for the police station. The police organized paint for their barracks. The women (who should be deported) persuaded the police until they got a few liters of paint, which they then used to paint their barracks. I do not think I have to mention that it was green color.

In the evening, when I was sitting outside with Suleiman again and we were looking at the women's hut, I asked him if he could remember our request. Astonished, a realization came over him.

These were just two examples of many at a time when I was still a long way from my current knowledge and state of being.

Meanwhile, I have managed not only familiar people like my wife, but also to heal strangers over long distances.

Even if I leave the house in the morning, I briefly think about what I need for the day and what resources are required for it.

I express briefly in my thoughts the desire to preserve these things and have achieved exactly this on my return.

Also, I always tell people in my presence that they should be careful what they want, because many things are fulfilled.

Like the story of a friend I helped to rebuild his house. We were in the not yet rebuilt basement and he said here would actually be space for a swimming pool. I laughed and warned him to be careful. Two days later there was a heavy storm and the cellar ran to a height of about 1.20 meters.

Everyone can and should think about these stories, but I can assure you that they happened the same way.

Every day a mantra

Let's get to the actual goal of this book.

"To change you and your life positively"

Who adheres to the instructions and disciplined applied the individual mantras for which everything will change. He will become calmer and more relaxed, he will be less in the daily fight and thus avoid a lot of stress and anger. His charisma becomes more loving and harmonious, his nature more friendly. It will also attract peace, harmony, love and happiness.

He loses fears and becomes more successful. Things will fall to him with (still) incomprehensible lightness. He increases his self-esteem and will calmly go to tasks that were far away for him until now. He will recognize his destiny, his way and the meaning of his existence.

Or in short: "He becomes a person who is deep in himself and to whom the success comes as a matter of course.

But everything has 2 pages, so of course the wish fulfillment. He will not succeed in hurting or injuring another, nor will he get (at least in the long term) what speaks against his purpose.

Take a few minutes each time for each mantra. I think that 5 minutes should be the minimum limit and recommend a time between 5-10 minutes. If it gets longer through meditation, that is also ok.

But even for someone without meditation experience is "Every day a mantra" suitable to achieve the results described above.

It is advisable to follow the order of the mantras for the first 45 days. They build on each other and serve to strengthen our positive energies and make negative ones disappear. After the first 45 days a lot will have changed for each one.

Learn the mantra by heart (should not be difficult, because I write them, except for syllabary and suffix, in English and keep it short.

After mastering the sentence, take a relaxed stance. This can be sitting or lying down. Try to relax and calm down. If that is difficult, focus on breathing until other things are hidden from the mind.

If this is achieved, "pray" now the mantra, that can be loud or just mental, or who wants to can sing it too. Repeat the mantra for 5-10 minutes (estimated, you do not need a watch for it). Then give a clear order or command to execution. For example, With the sentence "So be it" or "That's how it happens" Finally, thank the higher executive power.

The OM "Aum" (emphasis) may not always necessarily be recited, it is more to increase your own attention or concentration.

For the suffix "OM" you should make sure that both letters have the same length. So the emphasis of O is just as long as that of M.

Day 1

"OM - open my mind - OM"

"So be it, thank you"

It should and will be used to open our limited mind (limited by our conscious knowledge), in order to break down inner blockages, so that we learn to understand something that is still inexplicable for us.

Day 2

"OM - Let the light of your wisdom enter into me - OM"

"So be it, thank you"

In the light, that is, in the pure energy, everything is present, wisdom and knowledge, healing, love, peace, and things beyond the physical and psysical boundaries. Without a degree of wisdom and knowledge we will not be able to develop further.

Day 3

"OM - Work in me as my destiny foresees - OM"

"So be it, thank you"

No one will be able to escape his purpose. We always get hints on these. If we ignore these or act in the opposite direction, we will endure painful adversities until the hint comes again. The sooner we recognize and act accordingly, the less we will suffer and the less trouble for others.

Day 4

"OM - fill me with your love - OM"

"So be it, thank you"

Love is everything, everything is created out of love. The difference between being in love and love is enormous. (For more on these differences, see the "Book of Wisdom" and the "2nd Book of Wisdom")

Only when we recognize and strengthen the love that is in each one of us do we radiate it. What we radiate we attract. It is for example, someone who lovingly asks, as someone who asks or demands. Divine love is the food for our salvation.

Day 5

"OM - open my eyes and let me see - OM"

"So be it, thank you"

How often is our perspective characterized by experiences (mostly distressing) or by expectations and wanting or owning. We then walk through life with blinders blind to recognize the wonderful and beautiful things that are important to us. Sometimes we even run blind past our soulmate.

Day 6

"OM - let me feel - OM"

"So be it, thank you"

Many experiences make our feelings dull. How does the popular saying "have a thick coat" "stand above things" or "that's the way it is"

This is not completely wrong, but when we are so dulled that we can no longer allow feelings or want to live, we are actually dead, even if we live. Again, we do not allow beautiful things because we suppress our sensibility.

Day 7

"OM - let me hear - OM"

"So be it, thank you"

Be it hidden clues, cries of help from others, or the actual meaning of words that reach us or even our soul that very often says something to us, what we do not want to hear or hear.

Day 8

"OM teach me patience - OM"

"So be it, thank you"

One of the big problems of us humans is always the patience to wait for something. Impatience causes unrest and strife. They often lead to stomach problems.

Day 9

"OM - teach me compassion - OM"

"So be it, thank you"

Compassion, understanding (not to be confused with pity) is as important as love. They not only give and strengthen our strength, but also those of others. We will receive what we give, if necessary.

Day 10

"OM - teach me joy - OM"

"So be it, thank you"

Everyone knows the joy and knows what it means. Most people think that they do not have to learn joy, but what about the joy of the little things. To have enough to eat, a roof over your head to be healthy, the beauty of a flowering plant along the way?

But also joy when someone else is doing something beautiful or is fine, when he is helped out of necessity, we often live all this joy far too little and this is often like a stone that makes our hearts difficult without us recognizing this.

Day 11

"OM - teach me to recognize - OM"

"So be it, thank you"

Recognizing situations, consequences of actions, the meaning of what happens, without evaluating all of them. Evaluations always come from perspectives or experiences, are usually not neutral. They force us into patterns and often make us suffer.

Day 12

"OM - teach me to let that happen - OM"

"So be it, thank you"

We often try to forget or suppress unpleasant memories or experiences. It usually succeeds for a certain time, until something brings back this memory and again causes unrest, strife or an uneasy feeling.

Only with this will we be able to process them and later let them go so that they become what they are, namely, past.

Day 13

"OM - teach me to process that - OM"

"So be it, thank you"

Even the right processing needs to be learned. To persuade oneself that it does not matter will not help but to think that it was just fate. Processing has also to do with recognizing why, who acted in this situation, or it happened that way. Without looking for a guilt, neither with himself nor with others.

Day 14

"OM - teach me to let go - OM"

"So be it, thank you"

After allowing and processing we are in a position to let go.

See notes from day 12 and day 13.

Day 15

"OM - show me my destiny - OM"

"So be it, thank you"

Everything and everyone has a reason for its existence and also a task to fulfill. It is the determination of existence. For the most part, we do not know our destiny and err in our ways until we find and accept them. We can only become truly happy if we live according to our destiny.

Day 16

"OM - show me the way - OM"

"So be it, thank you"

The way to fulfill our destiny is usually dark for our consciousness. It is important not only to know the destiny but also the path that goes with it.

Day 17

"OM - give me courage - OM"

"So be it, thank you"

Many things that reach us on our way will scare us. But fear also has meaning, it will teach us mindfulness. Learning to overcome fear will strengthen our confidence and trust. It is courageous to continue on this path, no matter what.

Day 18

"OM - give me confidence - OM"

"So be it, thank you"

Even if we have the courage, self-doubt will often plague us, if we do everything right, if we can do it. That's why it's important to trust that everything happens as it should, that we are never burdened by our current limitations. Only when we have learned and mastered the respective level / lesson will there be the next enhancement or lesson.

Day 19

"OM - give me the food my soul needs - OM"

"So be it, thank you"

Not only body and mind, but also the soul wants to be nourished. What kind of food is needed in which moment, I can not write here as an author. It depends on the current state of affairs, the level of development and also on the respective destination. For example, a healer will need something different from a seer. Everyone will receive what they need.

Day 20

"OM - cleanse my heart - OM"

"So be it, thank you"

Feelings such as hatred or envy have to disappear from the heart if we truly want to be happy. It is not just about what we feel now, but also about what we did earlier, as a child or in a previous life (part of the primal guilt). All the negative we have experienced is like a dirt film on our hearts. True love will not feel comfortable in such a place, so the heart should be cleansed beforehand.

This mantra can be repeated more often, even in between. By listening to or reciting Gayatrimantra, the purification process can be strengthened and accelerated.

Day 21

"OM - help me find my peace and spread it - OM"

"So be it, thank you"

All things, situations with which we are not truly at peace, will return to our thinking. The true peace in us does not mean that we have already worked through everything and let go, but rather is the inner maturity to accept and process these things without evaluation. To make peace with it.

Once we have reached inner maturity, we radiate peace in all situations that come out. We convince in serenity. We convince in serenity, while others are already slightly panic. People who are still in conflict will seek our proximity.

Day 22

"OM - show me the inner balance - OM"

"So be it, thank you"

The inner balance and the inner peace is important so that we (as long as we are not yet valuation-free) can encounter unsightly things calmly and peacefully. But to much joy can blind us to danger. Who does not know the saying "Heaven-high, saddened to death" or has not yet experienced that came to a very successful high the big blow that triggered the opposite.

Day 23

"OM - Give me equanimity - OM"

"So be it, thank you"

Equanimity or the necessary serenity in everything that comes towards us, to consolidate and maintain our inner balance.

Day 24

"OM - Teach me valuation - OM"

"So be it, thank you"

Reviews are never neutral. Who lives in rating is not really tolerant. He will thereby attract for himself and for others discord. Anyone who is free of evaluation and living, also eludes the untrue importance of others' assessments about himself. He will thereby be able to live his destiny and feelings more confidently.

Day 25

"OM - Let love grow in me - OM"

"So be it, thank you"

It's all connected. Discord-peace, unhappiness - happiness, hate - love.

Those who have not truly found their inner peace will not be able to live in true love and thus can not really be happy. In this time, love is like a delicate plant that still needs care to develop into a beautiful flower.

Day 26

"OM - Let me live in truth - OM"

"So be it, thank you"

Being and living by yourself is difficult. Especially if you are afraid of consequences, be it professional or private. Often one tries to function and to fulfill expectations of others. One lives in lie of oneself. But also evaluations about events, the search for guilt is often a lie by our ego, because humans prefer to see a guilt with others than with themselves.

There is no wrong or right and thus no guilt, but only that does not understand truths.

Day 27

"OM - increase my innate abilities - OM"

"So be it, thank you"

Each of us has special abilities (I'm not talking about talents) that are outside our consciousness. These are the same in everyone. There is healing, seeing, soul whispering, channeling and much more. Which should now be particularly pronounced and used, will reveal itself with the recognition of its own purpose. But little hints arise before. One person can comfort and listen very well, the other one finds it easier to give practical help, just to give an example. In order to fulfill our own purpose, we will learn to increase our abilities.

Day 28

"OM - Enhance My Conscious Knowledge of the True Secrets - OM"

"So be it, thank you"

What are the true secrets? The innate abilities dormant within us, as well as understanding the true connections of things. Everything we do, or encountered, is directly related to other things. Not just cause and effect. The knowledge of these things will help us to change realities, it will lead us to success, make dreams come true.

Day 29

"OM - Give me confidence to apply my knowledge for the benefit of all - OM"

"So be it, thank you"

We can do a lot with our knowledge and skills. We will see many new things for us that will also scare us. For example, A healed person will for a while feel the fear that others will suffer from him and that is why he will suffer. But if he has understood what diseases really are and how to avert them, this fear will disappear.

Day 30

"OM - Let me endure patiently what happens to me - OM"

"So be it, thank you"

The higher the potential of our abilities and our knowledge, the more we want to effect. Sometimes that goes so far as we want to change the determination of another. That will not work, which sometimes is hard to take for one's self, especially when it's something we feel emotionally connected to.

Day 31

"OM - help me to recognize my original guilt - OM"

"So be it, thank you"

We are also rebirths of our ancestors. Everything that happened to them, everything they did is also present in us. I call it the original debt. If we can recognize these or gain knowledge about them, we have the opportunity to allow them to process and then let go.

Day 32

"OM - help me to get rid of my guilt - OM"

"So be it, thank you"

In order to eliminate our original guilt, that is, to process and let go are not only necessary to recognize, but also the knowledge and trust, sometimes endured necessary. With the help of the divine power, this will be easier for us.

Note: I deliberately chose two mantras for the 32nd day

Day 32

"OM - Let me find the Consciousness of True Love - OM"

"So be it, thank you"

True Love is a state of consciousness that no longer values. He is not focused on a person or object or anything. In this state of consciousness, one not only recognizes connections, one also knows the meaning of all and therefore will love everything, even that which according to human judgment is bad and evil.

Day 33

"OM - let me flow this true love - OM"

"So be it, thank you"

Even though we have attained the state of consciousness of true love, it will not always be easy to respond to everything and everyone with love, especially when we are at the very beginning of this love.

Day 34

"OM - lead me to my soulmate - OM"

"So be it, thank you"

Every living thing has a soulmate. Often they are separated from each other, due to circumstances or tasks that everyone has to fulfill. Let us guide, we will meet this. It is important that our heart and thinking is open, so that we recognize this.

Day 35

"OM - give me a laugh when the sadness comes over me - OM

"So be it, thank you"

Sometimes we are overcome by sadness. She takes us in those moments the joy of life, the strength to do our job. Everything is difficult in these moments. With a laugh, the sadness will take over the power to influence our actions. But sadness is also important because we appreciate the feeling of joy.

Day 36

"OM - help me make friends with me - OM"

"So be it, thank you"

Often we do things we do not want to do. The reasons are very different, but not important. It's always a struggle in us. In these moments, we do not like ourselves. Only when we also make friends with the "negative" sides in us can we succeed in turning these "negative" pages gradually away.

Day 37

"OM - help me to forgive myself - OM"

"So be it, thank you"

Friendship, inner peace, true love, but also "negative" sides, envy, hatred, etc. are interconnected. If we accept and recognize all this, we will no longer be angry with ourselves about so-called "mistakes" (which do not exist in the sense that they, too, have the purpose of learning), we can forgive these things in ourselves and to accept as part of us. This will enable us to change.

Day 38

"OM - help me forgive others - OM"

"So be it, thank you"

As long as our ego is not completely extinguished, we will live in evaluations. These cause us to look for guilt and often to find someone else. During this time, it is important to be able to forgive others, even if the other is not to blame, because it is only our point of view.

Day 39

"OM - give me joie de vivre, courage and life force - OM"

"So be it, thank you"

All that has been described before will bring strength and joy in the beginning, but also cost. It's not always easy to live like this because we have ego or desires that do not always agree with everyone, and yet it's the path everyone has to go sooner or later. We endure pain, grief and sorrow, suffer despondency, grief and listlessness. Sometimes we may see no point in all this.

Anyone who has taken part seriously here should now ask themselves the question "What has changed so far, how have I changed, how has my environment changed?

Day 40

"OM - Let me consciously perceive the changes - OM"

"So be it, thank you"

I am convinced that, no I know that in the past few days something has changed for everyone, that some mantras have already come true and that some may still need some time, so be patient.

Day 41

"OM - Let me continue to live in patience - OM"

"So be it, thank you"

For most people, a big change will be noticeable, their true nature will be more and more apparent, which is also perceived by their environment, which is changing as well.

Nevertheless, it is important to continue to be patient. I know the danger to want more and more, to move faster and faster. But everything comes only when you are ready and the time for it.

Impatience will lead to blockades and the already achieved partial and short-term lost.

Day 42

"OM - help me to become expectation free - OM"

"So be it, thank you"

I have meditated a long time on which point I should set this mantra.

Maybe I have already raised expectations at the beginning. Expectations are human, even if they are very often disappointed. In order to be able to implement expectation freedom, it requires a corresponding readiness, even a piece of road to inner peace should be behind one. With the knowledge and experience of the last 41 days, this is achieved and we can begin to reduce expectations.

Day 43

"OM - protect me from pride, delusion, anger and wrong views - OM"

"So be it, thank you"

Pride, lack of humility, delusion, anger, and wrong views almost always evoke evil or strife for themselves and others.

Day 44

"OM - protect me from jealousy, greed, envy and stinginess - OM"

"So be it, thank you"

Those who live in jealousy will always be looking for something that endangers their inner peace and thus is not truly happy. Greed and envy are also bad habits that one should get used to, because why should one get something that one begrudges others? Stinginess, holding on to have nothing to do with love, especially because they are often worldly things that are transient and not really important. But if one is ready to give or share, it will also be given to us. We will receive everything we need to live carefree.

Day 45

"OM - give me peace of mind - OM"

"So be it, thank you"

How often do we think what will be tomorrow, if I have enough to eat tomorrow, stay healthy, my loved ones stay healthy and are with me or if I can keep my roof over my head, in my own unease, in doubt.

These worries only take place in our thinking. If we live in love, humility, trust and mindfulness, we need not worry about these things, because we will receive or find everything, we will be given everything we need.

More mantras for all situations

From now on, the order of the mantras no longer needs to be considered. They can be freely chosen according to the needs of each individual. I try to list them in individual categories like love, peace, health and wish fulfillment. Likewise I will omit the "OM", the order "So be it" and the thanksgiving. But do not forget to use them when reciting, especially when it comes to orders and thanksgiving.

If you notice what sometimes happens to one or the other, that you fall back into old patterns or into negative feelings like envy, greed, jealousy, expectation or anything else, go back to the first 45 days, look for the appropriate one and recite the matching mantra again. Likewise, you should get used to observing your behavior or actions so that you can not please, work against. Because I want to make a long-term change to love or peace. Not just to fulfill a short-term desire. This would be dishonest towards yourself and calculating, as well as rating.

General

"Support me to believe in the good"

"Give me a happy future"

"Give me satisfaction"

"Help me to remember those who give thanks every day for what you have given me"

"Give me what I need"

"Always keep my hope upright"

"Give what you give me to everyone else"

"As you help me to recognize, help others too

"Let me do what is necessary for the benefit of all"

"Am I mistaken in darkness, lead me into the light?"

"Always leave me a smile and a comforting word for the one who needs it"

"Solve my limits in the head"

"Remove my blockages"

"Give me answers to the questions, as well as to questions the answers"

"Help me to feel the imperfect"

"Give me purity, faithfulness, creativity and enlightenment"

"Let my thoughts always be honest and true"

"Let me see the sun, even when it rains"

"Give me time for the important things"

"Leave me where I am needed"

"Teach me to renounce humbly"

"Let my arms be open to receive happiness"

"Let my dreams become reality"

"Inspire my imagination"

"Lead me to the fork of life"

"Let me recognize all honest words"

"Show me who I am"

"Show me why I am"

"Let me see and taste the colors of life"

"Give me gentleness and tolerance for other views"

"Let all my levels of consciousness resonate in harmony"

"Let me know that I'm never alone"

"Let me out of the stones that meet me build bridges"

"Show me the secrets of all universes and states of being"

"Help me to live up to my responsibilities to myself and others"

"Let me always make the best of the circumstances"

"Help me to do the right thing"

"Let me share and give joy"

"Always let me find time for my friends"

"Free me from the assessment in hard and easy"

"Let me start and finish everything at the right time"

"Give me the courage to go through thick and thin with friends"

"Let me go, if I have to go, let me wait, if I have to wait and let myself rest, if I need rest"

"Give me the right words in due time"

"Let me know that everything is possible"

"Let me understand how everything is possible"

"Give me a flexible mind and perspective"

"Give me mindfulness for what I do not know consciously"

"Let me look behind the meaning of the experience"

"Let me recognize the transience of situations and objects"

"Help me with my thought journeys"

"Show me and let me understand"

"Let me be happy in simplicity, too"

"Let my inner beauty blossom like a flower to give pleasure to others with my sight"

"Give me motivation"

"Help me to honestly check my mindset and my actions"

"Give me courage to go through dark doors, even though they scare me"

"Let me see the wonderful things hidden in the shadows"

"Let me just radiate what I want to wear"

"Make everyday happy days for me and others"

"Give me the right doubt at the right moment"

"Let me share in the wonderful coincidence of things"

"Keep the child in me"

"Let me be a worthy role model for others"

"Let me rest in time and pause to enjoy beautiful"

"Let me feel with all life fibers"

"Free me from self-lying"

"Let me take advantage of my patience that is possible"

"Let me breathe consciously"

"Give me encounters with others to exchange experiences"

"Help me to accept how everything is"

"Help me to gain awareness"

"Always let me react and act understandingly"

"Lead me to those who need me and whom I need"

"Let me always be home, no matter where I am"

"Release me from old ways of thinking"

"Give me joy on the joy of others"

"Give me self-sufficiency"

"Let others share in my happiness, too"

"Extend my mental horizon"

"Catch me when I fall or fall"

"Let me overcome my ego"

"Give me the change for the better"

"Let me only promise what I can fulfill"

"Give me courage and confidence to face all dangers"

"Let me respect the diversity of all"

"Help me to swing everything together"

"Let me perceive and react appropriately"

"Let me serve others with joy"

"Give me the strength to work on my inner values"

"Let me find what's in me"

"Help me to overcome my ego"

"Let my mind be quiet and silence, so that everything can come to me"

"Let me recognize my inner spaces"

"Help me to enter my inner rooms"

"Let me inhale all the wonderful scents.

"Let me do all the things that are important"

"Help me to make the little things with great love"

"Help me to recognize the ways"

"Give me the courage to follow the paths without hesitation"

"Retrieve me from the suffering of my expectations"

"Give me the right words, where words are needed"

"Make every day the best day of my life so far"

"Let me make the most of my actions"

"Give me understanding, if I need understanding"

"Give me compassion when I need compassion"

"Protect me in all my actions"

"Protect me in all my ways"

"Protect my family"

"Protect anyone who is in danger"

Love

"Let me live love"

"Let my heart swing"

"Let me hear the call of my soulmate"

"Protect my sweetheart (s)"

"Let me understand the miracle of love"

"Help me to become expectant"

"Let me love unconditionally"

"Help me to let go of my love"

"Help me to accept love"

"Let me feel the love of my soulmate in my sleep"

"Let my soulmate feel my love in his sleep, too"

"Give us the necessary soul hugs and kisses"

"Seal and protect our love"

"Help me out of the legacy of the disappointments of building bridges of love"

"Help me climb the steps of our suffering so we are better"

"I am with you and in you, just like you with me, because we are one"

"Let me read in the soul of my partner, so that I understand better"

"Let me know that I'm never alone"

"I feel your hand groping for mine, let us float away from all the worldly."

"Help me to overcome my shyness"

"Let love warm my heart every day"

"Let me slide in the river of love, whether gentle or roaring and rushing"

"Help me to act in silence, unnoticed by others"

"Give me the drop of love that is greater than all the oceans"

"Let me always find the fruit of love as I need it"

"I appear in your dreams to get your attention"

"My heart will always call for you to find me"

"Eternally take my strength from your love"

"Draw your strength forever from my love"

"Feel my love for you forever"

"Let me feel your love for me forever"

"Give my soul warmth when you are cold"

"Give my soul a smile when she is sad"

"Let everything be as it should be"

"Always be there for me"

"I am always there for you"

"Give life to my party spirit"

"Give us enough erotic moments"

"Put my love in the necessary vibrations"

"Let's always give each other what the other one needs"

"Always give me the feeling of being close to you"

"Give him / her the feeling of being near me"

"Let each other be our angels"

"Let us go hand in hand through the storms of life"

"Let our hearts swing in unison"

"Let's enjoy the wonderful of our love"

"Join and bring together what belongs together"

"Let me overcome my ego for our love"

"My strength, my spirit and the energy of my love should always accompany you"

"Let me share my tenderness"

"Give me the strength to always be there for the lonely"

"Let me accept his / her tenderness"

"Lead my soulmate to me, like me to him"

"Let me find my soulmate again when he / she has changed the state of being"

"Let me feel the breath of love"

"Let the thoughts of my love fly to her / him"

"Always let me react appropriately with love"

"Let me always work on our love"

"Let me recognize the magic of our love"

"Let's keep silent where words are superfluous"

"I want you to be fine"

"I want to go through life with you hand in hand"

"I want to dance with you through the rain"

"In our love let the water taste sweet as honey"

"Let our happiness arise and grow in us"

"Let my thinking become calm and quiet so that love can come to me"

"Let me taste the wonderful scents of love"

"Let my soulmate feel my yearning"

"Fulfill my yearning"

"Let me feel heaven on earth"

"Let my thoughts of love be like a rock in the surf"

"Let me do all the things that are important to true love"

"Let me recognize and walk the paths of true love"

"Keep the sorrow of my expectations far from my love"

"Protect our love"

"Protect my life partner"

"Give everyone safety when they are in danger of losing themselves"

Health

"Let me see the causes"

"Give me my answers, the right questions"

"Give me well-being"

"Help me to change the perceived reality of diseases"

"Let me endure the pain and sorrow in me"

"Help me to accept pain and suffering"

"Help me to understand pain and suffering"

"Help me to let go of pain and suffering"

"Give me a healthy look"

"Protect my aura and soul before and under stress"

"Let me see and taste the colors of health"

"Strengthen my inner peace and solve my illnesses"

"Help me climb the steps of my suffering so I feel better."

"Free me from my original guilt"

"Take the strife in me, the power to bring me disease"

"Let my tears wash away the sorrow and the pain"

"Free me from the trouble that makes me sick"

"Help me to get well and give me healing sleep"

"Let me make new decisions for the sake of my health"

"Let me find the existing healing words of kindness.

"Give me joie de vivre and life force when I need it"

"Keep your protective light on me"

"Let me overcome the causes of my ego"

"Be the change from illness to health"

"Let me breathe in your health and exhale the disease"

"Give me courage and confidence"

"Let me feel the magic of your healing power"

"Let me use the magic of your healing power"

"Let my soul hand hold the hand of the lonely, if they must be afraid or change the state of being alone"

"Let my mental injuries heal, so that I can also recover physically"

"Let me and the vibrations of healing harmonize"

"Help me on suffering to respond appropriately with love"

"Help me to overcome my illnesses"

"Keep my mind calm and still, so that recovery can come to me"

"Let me breathe in the wonderful healing fragrances"

"Let me do all the things that are important to my health"

"Let me see the ways to well-being and health"

"Reduce my need for doctor visits"

"Reduce the need for medication"

"Make me healthier every day"

"Dissolve and extinguish pathological bitterness in me"

"Protect me from diseases"

"Give me recovery"

"Give me the courage to free others from their illness"

"Show me the way and the solutions to free others from their illness"

Peace

"Give me the serenity to start the day offhandedly"

"Let me meet every day with joy and harmony"

"Help me to become judgment free"

"Protect me from carelessness"

"Free me from dependencies"

"Let me understand the souls of all beings"

"Let me accept with peace what you have prepared for me"

"Help me to remember what strife means to me.

"Help me balance positive and negative"

"Let me understand recurring lessons"

"Strengthen my love and trust when doubts want to gain the upper hand"

"Free me from my primal fault of dissatisfaction"

"Let my tears wash away strife"

"Help me live in harmony and peace with everyone and everything"

"Help me climb the steps of all sorrow so that I can work for peace"

"Let me and my thoughts be like a rock in the surf for peace"

"Let me realize that hopeless situations are transitory"

"Let me be the light for others to recognize"

"Give me carefreeness"

"Let me feel the magic of your peace"

"Always let me work on my peace"

"Let the peace arise and grow in me"

"Help me to let love and peace flow until all envy and hatred have passed"

"Give me the courage and the freedom to choose my thoughts without fear"

"Give me a life beyond good and evil"

"Help me to forgive me and others"

"Give me a soul smile when the sadness comes"

"Give me the carefreeness of a child"

"Let me overcome my ego for peace"

"Be the change and let me be the change to peace"

"Always let the breath of peace be around me"

"Let me face all dangers with courage, confidence and serenity"

"Give me and my family, peace and harmony in our environment"

"Always let the sun shine for me, regardless of the weather"

"Help me reach many with my peaceful vibrations"

"Let me see discord and respond appropriately with love"

"Help me overcome my strife"

"Let my thinking be quiet and quiet so peace can come to me"

"Let me inhale the scents of peace"

"Let me do all the things that are important for peace"

"Show me the way to peace and freedom"

"Solve and extinguish the bitterness that disturbs peace"

"Help me to follow this path unswervingly"

"Give me the understanding of peace in me"

"Give me compassion in times of strife"

"Protect my actions I do for peace"

"Protect all who work in peace"

"Give my family peace"

"Give me the tolerance for those who are still in trouble"

"Show me the solutions to free others from their strife"

"Give me the courage to free others from their strife"

"Give my friends peace"

"Let my family always live in peace"

"Show everyone how they can live in peace"

"Protect all who are in danger of losing their peace"

Wish fulfillment and success

"I can do that, I can do it, I do that"

"Help me out (at this point the respective situation)"

"Let me enjoy the transient until it is time to pass away"

"Let me find a job that suits my purpose"

"Show me the way to a carefree life"

"Show me the way to success"

"Change my reality as I wish it“

"Give me prosperity"

"Let my seed flourish and grow"

"Let me share and give joy to my prosperity"

"Give me the confidence to achieve everything"

(here you can call individual things directly for everything)

"Give me motivation"

"Help me to recognize my chances"

"Lead me to the winning side"

"Let me reap what I sowed"

"Let me overcome my ego of greed and envy"

"Be the change and let me be the change to success"

"Let me inhale the energy that I need for success"

"Give me the interview during job interviews, which I consider important for the respective company"

"Let me always give the best"

"Let grow small and big easy"

"Let everything be as it should be"

"Always let me work on my success"

"Let the success arise and grow in me"

You have now met 370 mantras, which you can apply gradually, depending on where something pushes or moves you. Of course, you can also apply each mantra specifically to an event or situation. You can insert names or labels.

I think or should I say better, I'm convinced that with the current knowledge you can also create one or the other smaller mantra for yourself.

But again this reminder: never use the words no, not, never, nothing, etc.

Light and love for you

I want to bring you 365 more wisdom and insights. From personalities like Buddha, Gandhi, Mother Theresa and many others, as well as from me K.Wirtz Bodhisattva.

A wisdom for every day

Do not believe anything because a sage said it

Do not believe anything because it's written

Do not believe anything because it is considered sacred

Do not believe anything because someone else believes

Only believe what you have recognized as true.

Buddha

You should not judge others because they have a different view than you do. But you should try to understand other points of view, because this will allow us to expand our consciousness.

K.Wirtz Bodhisattva

Good can never come from lies and violence

Mahatma Gandhi

All doors of life are open to you, you just have to go through it even if you can not see clearly what's behind it, do not be afraid.

K.Wirtz Bodhisattva

All cruelty springs from weakness.

Lucius Annaeus Seneca

Even in the shade, wonderful things are often present. You should have the courage to see them.

K.Wirtz Bodhisattva

In a sea of pain, some drown. The others learn to swim in it.

Kyrilla Spiecker

Suffering is nothing more than a dependence on something, we are beyond evaluation, expectation and ego, we can let go and suffering is not existent.

K.Wirtz Bodhisattva

It is important to listen to his inner feeling.

K.Wirtz Bodhisattva

A drop of love is more than an ocean mind.

Blaise Pascal

Living in inner peace and balance means being free.

K.Wirtz Bodhisattva

Happiness does not dwell in possession and not in gold, the happiness is at home in the soul.

Democritus

What you radiate attracts you.

K.Wirtz Bodhisattva

The most incomprehensible thing about the universe is that we can understand it.

Albert Einstein

You can make every day your lucky day in which you or someone else a joy.

K.Wirtz Bodhisattva

The Human is a part of nature and not something that contradicts it.

Bertrand Russel

Meditation or just one to focus and intensify his love and happiness.

K.Wirtz Bodhisattva

Man can experience miracles only when he is ready to open his heart and eyes to them.

Augustine of Hippo

Sometimes it is important to have a tiny moment of doubt in your knowledge because it draws attention to the fact that nothing is taken for granted.

K.Wirtz Bodhisattva

Man finally wants to get as far as the flowers and the trees: live quietly and die. No doubt most people do not want anything better.

Christian Morgenstern

In his feelings, there is no wrong or right. Appraisals often lead to cramping and no longer honest living of his feelings.

K.Wirtz Bodhisattva

Most people are as happy as they have themselves.

Abraham Lincoln

If new questions arise through a knowledge gained, remain calm and try not to find convulsive / compulsive answers.

K.Wirtz Bodhisattva

A life without joy is like a long journey without a guesthouse.

Democritus

You should never say what you do not mean, it brings inner dissatisfaction, if not worse.

K.Wirtz Bodhisattva

A truly great man will neither crush a worm nor crawl before the emperor.

Benjamin Franklin

You should devote all your time to everything, especially yourself.

K.Wirtz Bodhisattva

Experience is not what happens to you. Experience is what you make of what happens to you.

Aldous Huxley

Take care of your carefreeness.

K.Wirtz Bodhisattva

It is tremendous luck to be able to be happy.

Georg Bernhard Shaw

It is always amazing to see how things fit in with serenity.

K.Wirtz Bodhisattva

It is not enough to know, you also have to apply.

Johann Wolfgang von Goethe

From time to time you should take your hand and show what you have forgotten in your mind.

K.Wirtz Bodhisattva

Joy of the joy and suffering of the suffering of others are the best leaders of humanity.

Albert Einstein

To practice patience and serenity is a great challenge for many.

K.Wirtz Bodhisattva

Give every day a chance to become the most beautiful of your life.

Mark Twain

How often do people feel betrayed by our actions because they have a different view, how often do we feel betrayed?

K.Wirtz Bodhisattva

The less one needs, the more he approaches the gods, who need nothing at all.

Socrates

The sooner and further one expands one's consciousness and point of view, the less suffering one will attach to oneself and to others.

K.Wirtz Bodhisattva

Mediocre spirits usually condemn everything that goes beyond their horizon.

Francois Duc de La Rochefoucauld

Anyone can try (perhaps with temporary success) to escape his ultimately positive destiny because his ego sees it differently, but it will not work in the long run.

K.Wirtz Bodhisattva

What people do for love always happens beyond good and evil.

Friedrich Nietzsche

How important is time, day or night really, as opposed to light, love, peace and health?

K.Wirtz Bodhisattva

What you are depends on three factors: what you have inherited, what your environment has made of you, and what you have freely chosen from your environment and your heritage.

Aldous Huxley

Give all things their time that is needed. You can shout at the apple to grow faster, but he probably will not do it.

K.Wirtz Bodhisattva

How numerous are the things that I do not need.

Socrates

Often, experiences, situations return and it is up to each one himself how he encounters them. If you refuse the change, it leads to dissatisfaction and repetition until you understand.

K.Wirtz Bodhisattva

If the state of the soul changes, so does the appearance of the body and vice versa: if the appearance of the body changes, so does the state of the soul.

Aristotle

Let yourself be guided in the flow of love, sometimes gently gliding, sometimes rushing and rushing.

K.Wirtz Bodhisattva

The greatest wealth is self-sufficiency. The greatest fruit of self-sufficiency is independence.

Epicurus

Do things because you like them, aware of possible consequences, let go of fear because in the end not important.

K.Wirtz Bodhisattva

Not by tearing the blossom, you will capture its beauty.

Rabindranath Tagore

Where there is a will, there is a way. If you do not want to (right) you are usually on a wrong path.

K.Wirtz Bodhisattva

Nothing is easier than to deceive oneself; because what we want, we willingly believe.

Demosthenes

If peace and love ripen in you like a delicate little plant, take care of it and do not tear the smallest roots out of the way.

K.Wirtz Bodhisattva

There is a fulfilling life despite many unfulfilled wishes.

Dietrich Bonhoeffer

Lack of trust often leads to wanting to control everything, thus curtailing the freedom of another who will eventually break out.

K.Wirtz Bodhisattva

As nothing is too great for the spirit, goodness is nothing too small.

Jean Paul

Conditions, expectations often foster fears that allow us to be biased, disappointed.

K.Wirtz Bodhisattva

It's nice to see your own image in the loving eye.

Johann Wolfgang von Goethe

Between fears, hope, despair but also joy, I have found peace and therefore I do not want to miss a day.

K.Wirtz Bodhisattva

If love prevailed on earth, all laws would be dispensable.

Aristotle

Peace, happiness, love and health are the most precious goods.

K.Wirtz Bodhisattva

It is not happy who happens to others, but who considers himself to be.

Seneca

Sometimes it is better to work in silence and with a smile on the success achieved, even if the one does not notice.

K.Wirtz Bodhisattva

If we can make a person happier, we should definitely do it, may he ask us or not.

Hermann Hesse

Let love and peace flow until envy and hate are washed away.

K.Wirtz Bodhisattva

As the excess of joy often ends in sadness, new pleasures follow the suffering that has been overcome.

Giovanni Boccaccio

You never know exactly how things would have turned out if you had decided otherwise. Therefore one can rarely say that one has not decided correctly.

K.Wirtz Bodhisattva

Holding on to his anger is like picking up a glowing coal and throwing it at someone.

Buddha

Do you have something for you to recognize as right or truthful trade after that, even though there are always many others who speak against it.

K.Wirtz Bodhisattva

We believe we have experiences, but experiences make us.

Eugène Ionesco

Now and then pause to enjoy the beautiful, detached from the fear of missing something.

K.Wirtz Bodhisattva

What you say to me, I forget. I remember what you have shown me. What you let me do, I understand.

Confucius

Why should I condemn what others think / say about me? They have different experiences / truths or ways.

K.Wirtz Bodhisattva

Holding on to anger is like drinking poison and waiting for the other to die from it.

Buddha

No matter what others say or think about you in their dissatisfaction, you are you and so willed by something higher.

K.Wirtz Bodhisattva

Sometimes the shackles that keep us from being free are more mental than real

Author unknown

In our senses we are as different as the elements. Accordingly, the paths are just as different. Only the goal of love, remains the same.

K.Wirtz Bodhisattva

Watch your thoughts, for they will become your destiny.

Buddha

All that one misses in reality, in another self-created reality with all the fibers of life.

K.Wirtz Bodhisattva

Do not rely on the opinion of others and do not seek excessive fame. Look carefully and make your own judgment.

Nagarjuna

Always there for those in need, it would be easy to close your eyes / ears and hands, but the price would be your own happiness and peace.

K.Wirtz Bodhisattva

By frivolity you lose the roots, by restlessness the overview.

Lao Tzu

Sometimes when a circle / cycle closes there is no turning back.

K.Wirtz Bodhisattva

Rest brings balance and lightness, balance and ease bring inner peace and serenity.

Chuang Tzu

Something necessarily compulsive hold want brings loss fears with it.

K.Wirtz Bodhisattva

Real happiness requires peace of mind or a measure of spiritual serenity. If this exists, hardness matters nothing. With inner strength or mental stability, we can bear all kinds of adversities.

Dalai Lama

Only those who know the deepest suffering can recognize what true happiness is and means.

K.Wirtz Bodhisattva

Find your own wisdom in yourself.

Padmasambhawa

Even if you have let go of everything, it does not mean you have no wishes and goals.

K.Wirtz Bodhisattva

Life has many detours in it. The art is to admire the landscape.

Zen wisdom

Insights come step by step, often unnoticed at first, until they snatch one, the reality that has been felt so far and nothing is the way it was.

K.Wirtz Bodhisattva

Water solidifies to ice, ice melts into water. What is born dies again; what has died is alive again. Water and ice are ultimately one. Life and death, both are good.

Zen wisdom

If I think I'm scared, I'm scared. I think shame I feel shame etc. Be what you are and live the feelings no matter what others think.

K.Wirtz Bodhisattva

The teaching is like a raft used to cross a river to the other shore, but left behind and unable to carry around with it when it has served its purpose.

Buddha

When you approach the end of the state of consciousness of true love, you come to a point of "being" where you are.

K.Wirtz Bodhisattva

You smile - and the world is changing.

Buddha

Do not fulfill your greatest wish today, do not be sad, but look forward to tomorrow.

K.Wirtz Bodhisattva

The seeds of the past are the fruits of the future.

Buddha

If for no reason a euphoric feeling of happiness flows through you, it means inner peace.

K.Wirtz Bodhisattva

Each one of us is a god. Each of us is omniscient. All we have to do is open our consciousness to listen to our own wisdom.

Buddha

To see how a vibration changes the fabric of its existence and becomes the sound of the ultimate truth of eternal "being."

K.Wirtz Bodhisattva

If you want to know who you were, look who you are. If you want to know who you will be, look what you are doing.

Buddha

Mindfulness in one's actions can increase self-esteem.

K.Wirtz Bodhisattva

The best prayer is patience.

Buddha

Only the human constantly thinks about why and misses many beautiful opportunities.

K.Wirtz Bodhisattva

Violation of living beings, lying and slander avoids and abhors the righteous. He speaks the truth and is helpless against the people. He speaks words that create harmony.

Buddha

Without being conscious of oneself, one will not be able to recognize one's own truthfulness and will live in self-lying.

K.Wirtz Bodhisattva

I call the will the action, for if the will is there, it works, be it in works, words or thoughts.

Buddha

It never works everything you do or want to do. But if you doubt before, you should not even try it.

K.Wirtz Bodhisattva

Looking at life in detail, it is possible to see clearly everything that is. Enslaved by nothing, it is possible to let go of all desires. The result is a life of joy and peace. That is, really living alone.

Buddha

Every stone that gets in our way is a chapter in the textbook of life.

K.Wirtz Bodhisattva

Learn to let go. That's the key to happiness.

Buddha

The path to inner peace is not as difficult as most people think. Surely, the inner authority, patience, humility as well as practice, meditation and the belief that everything is possible.

K.Wirtz Bodhisattva

Happiness is in us, not in things.

Buddha

Anger that we usually associate with things is annoying about ourselves. It is our expectations that we have and that are not fulfilled.

K.Wirtz Bodhisattva

More wonderful than all happiness on earth or in heaven, greater than the mastery of the whole world is the joy of the first step on the path of enlightenment.

Buddha

Anger can make us ill, cause anger or sadness, can lead us to be unfair to ourselves and others.

K.Wirtz Bodhisattva

Man suffers because he desires to possess and retain things that are transient in nature.

Buddha

In the spiritual, nothing can be achieved by force. If one forces oneself it often goes wrong or one does not feel nice experiences and frustration comes in, which leads in turn to it no longer to try and give up.

K.Wirtz Bodhisattva

He who knows is not in doubt.

Buddha

There are no limits if we are free to think.

K.Wirtz Bodhisattva

Observe yourself and do not depend on others.

Buddha

Likewise, it is advisable to share with others about the experience. It gives us self-affirmation and courage in our doing. Also, we can learn from other experiences or teach.

K.Wirtz Bodhisattva

Words have the power to destroy or heal. When words are true and yet benevolent, they can change our world.

Buddha

There is no right or wrong. Only things that bring us faster than others.

K.Wirtz Bodhisattva

Do not look for the truth, just stop having an opinion about everything.

Zen Bhuddism

Sharpen your senses. We have eyes to see, ears to hear, fingers to feel, sense of taste and thinking. For example, The blind accepted by the simple that he can not see and thus has simply better trained his other senses.

K.Wirtz Bodhisattva

The most important science in the world, in heaven and on earth - is love.

Mother Theresa

Everything that happens to us, what we experience, others have already experienced and will experience more after us.

K.Wirtz Bodhisattva

Hungry is not just about bread. Much more bitter is the hunger for love.

Mother Theresa

Everything negative also has a positive side, you just have to learn to see and use it for yourself.

K.Wirtz Bodhisattva

The worst poverty is loneliness and the feeling of being unnoticed and unwanted.

Mother Theresa

If you smile at someone you usually get a smile back. That also applies to fate.

K.Wirtz Bodhisattva

We will never know how much good a simple smile can accomplish.

Mother Theresa

Being able to give conditions to love, it will remain forever.

K.Wirtz Bodhisattva

It is easy to love distant people. But it is not always easy to love those who live next door to us.

Mother Theresa

If someone really loves you and you love him, you will not break anything in the long run.

K.Wirtz Bodhisattva

I've experienced the paradox that if I love until it hurts, there's no pain left, just love.

Mother Theresa

It's just important what others think about you when you compare their views with yours and gain insight into what you can improve for yourself.

K.Wirtz Bodhisattva

Love is a fruit that always has season, and anyone can pick from it as much as he wants.

Mother Theresa

Never think that you are not needed just because in self-pity everything becomes too much for you.

K.Wirtz Bodhisattva

Patience is a tree whose root is bitter, but whose fruit is very sweet.

Chinese proverb

Even if you seem to be further in your state of development than another, be patient with yourself and the other.

K.Wirtz Bodhisattva

When you realize that you want nothing, the whole world is yours.

Lao Tzu

Never seek guilt neither from yourself nor from others. Blame is usually only judgment from a single point of view and thus will not contribute to the solution of the problem.

K.Wirtz Bodhisattva

The world is full of little joys, the art is only to see them.

Chinese proverb

The search for guilt in others often only serves the purpose of calming one's conscience.

K.Wirtz Bodhisattva

The lucky ones regret the brevity of the days, the sad ones tire of the sneaking of the years. But who is free from joy and suffering, for which is not "short" or "long" time.

Asian wisdom

Even though we are so tiny, unlike the Universe, like a grain of sand on the beach, we are so great as to bring forth or alter universes with a tiny sliver of ours.

K.Wirtz Bodhisattva

There is no gateway to happiness or misfortune; both come when you invite them.

from Japan

You can only forgive yourself, because disappointments or injuries are just the unfulfilled expectations you put.

K.Wirtz Bodhisattva

Spouses who love each other say a thousand things without speaking.

Chinese proverb

Even a day without special success is not a lost day.

K.Wirtz Bodhisattva

Goodness in words generates trust, goodness in thought generates depth, goodness in giving generates love.

Lao Tzu

Also enjoy small things, even if they seem natural to you. Nothing is self-evident.

K.Wirtz Bodhisattva

All rivers flow into the sea. All things point in one direction.

Far Eastern wisdom

Just because you do not consciously perceive many things does not mean that it does not exist in you.

K.Wirtz Bodhisattva

Make life and death equally important, and your mind will be without fear.

Lao Tzu

We meet people who accompany us a piece of life because we have the same way for a while. Even if we split then they will meet us again at the destination. Because the goal is the same in the end.

K.Wirtz Bodhisattva

Almost everything you do is, in the end, unimportant. But it is important that you do it.

Mahatma Gandhi

We do not die, we only change our state of being. We were at the beginning and will be at the end as well as everything because we are everything.

K.Wirtz Bodhisattva

The serene uses his chance better than the driven.

from China

Once you have found your inner peace as a human, it will be your home until your state of being changes. No matter where you are.

K.Wirtz Bodhisattva

A no of deepest conviction is better and greater than a yes that is said only to please or to avoid difficulties.

Mahatma Gandhi

The past is not important, it has passed and can not be changed. What is important is what you have learned and use in the present.

K.Wirtz Bodhisattva

What you think about the summit is just one step.

from China

Also what you have done in the past is not important, but what you do now.

K.Wirtz Bodhisattva

If time is not ripe, nothing can happen; when it is ripe, nothing can prevent it.

from China

In sleep we recover best, because the inner power without conscious distraction (which we have in the waking state) works better on us.

K.Wirtz Bodhisattva

May your worst day of the future be better than your best of the past.

Lao Tzu

We call miracles what we can not explain with our human minds.

K.Wirtz Bodhisattva

Who leads may not stand in the way of those whom he leads.

Lao Tzu

In another state of consciousness these miracles are just circumstances.

K.Wirtz Bodhisattva

Fear not slow forward, just be afraid of standing still

Asian wisdom

Insights reach us only as much and as strong as we can handle them without getting sick.

K.Wirtz Bodhisattva

If you stop every time a dog barks, you will never finish your journey.

Arabic proverb

Nothing is as constant as the change, even if much seems the same, it is different, often unnoticed.

K.Wirtz Bodhisattva

By moving one overcomes cold. Silence overcomes heat. The wise man, through his purity and tranquility, is able to balance all things in the world.

Lao Tzu

I always have the freedom to choose my thoughts.

K.Wirtz Bodhisattva

Treat each other's faults with as much leniency as your own.

Chinese proverb

I make new and different choices that are more helpful and healthy for me.

K.Wirtz Bodhisattva

Nothing does as much harm as anger, and nothing brings more benefit than patience.

from China

I am ready to break away from those patterns of thinking that contributed to the emergence of a situation.

K.Wirtz Bodhisattva

No food is cooked and no bread is baked without fire, and yet man wants to mature without suffering.

Chinese proverb

The state of consciousness of true love means to let love flow without judgment into everything and everyone.

K.Wirtz Bodhisattva

The ocean does not know complete peace, so does the ocean of life.

Mahatma Gandhi

Caught in the freedom of true love.

K.Wirtz Bodhisattva

Do not blame the river if you fall into the water.

Jean Jaurès

When I have changed my current state of being, I am still connected to every single one I encountered in my life.

K.Wirtz Bodhisattva

Turn great difficulties into small and small into none.

from China

If you live in the dependence on habits, it's hard to find a new way to happiness. Have courage and dissolve.

K.Wirtz Bodhisattva

If you have suffered enough, you will bring yourself to the point that changes everything.

Buddhist wisdom

Even during our lifetime, we die many small deaths, because every change is also a death of the past.

K.Wirtz Bodhisattva

Look at nature: it is constantly in action, never standing still, yet silent.

Mahatma Gandhi

As we change our way of thinking and seeing, we are able to influence and change our reality.

K.Wirtz Bodhisattva

On the quiet river, the shore is full of flowers.

Chinese proverb

The most beautiful thing we can experience is the mysterious.

Albert Einstein

If we accept the knowledge of our levels of consciousness, we will be able to learn and apply it.

K.Wirtz Bodhisattva

You should be grateful for the least, and you will be worthy to receive greater things.

Thomas à Kempis

Earlier, expectant, I struggled for the unattainable and had nothing but pain, letting love flow today and all I need is to come to me.

K.Wirtz Bodhisattva

Let us be thankful to people who make us happy. They are the lovable gardeners who make our soul bloom.

Marcel Proust

I enjoy everything in peace and let me even pass by a snail, the time and speed is relative.

K.Wirtz Bodhisattva

Humility is really nothing more than a comparison of its value with moral perfection.

Immanuel Kant

Every living thing has a soulmate. Often they are separated from each other, due to circumstances or tasks that everyone has to fulfill. Let us guide, we will meet this. It is important that our hearts and minds are open so that we recognize them.

K.Wirtz Bodhisattva

If a problem can be solved, why be unhappy? And if it can not be solved, then why be unhappy?

ZenWeisheit

Those who live in jealousy will constantly search for something that endangers their inner peace and thus is not truly happy.

K.Wirtz Bodhisattva

Be, not try to become one.

Osho

If we live in love, humility, trust and mindfulness, we are worry-free.

K.Wirtz Bodhisattva

See things as they are.

Buddha

What are the true secrets? The innate capacities that dormant within us, as well as the understanding of the true connections of things. Everything we do, or encountered, is directly related to other things. Not just cause and effect.

K.Wirtz Bodhisattva

Die while you live and be completely dead. Then do whatever you want - everything is fine.

Zenkai Shibayama

The world always has beautiful things and is full of wonders. It is not their fault if you are blind in strife

K.Wirtz Bodhisattva

In love, little gestures are more than big words.

Marcel Baumert

Even the right processing needs to be learned. To persuade oneself that it does not matter will help as well as to think that it was just fate. Processing has also to do with recognizing why, who acted in this situation, or did it so. Without looking for a guilt, neither with himself nor with others.

K.Wirtz Bodhisattva

We spend our lives waiting for the extraordinary, instead of transforming the ordinary people around us.

Hans Urs von Balthasar

Everything and everyone has a reason for its existence and also a task to fulfill. It is the determination of existence.

K.Wirtz Bodhisattva

If the sun does not wait for praise and requests to rise, but is lit and welcomed by the whole world, you may not need flattery or applause to do good. By yourself you must do it: then you will be loved like the sun.

Epiket

We can only become truly happy if we live according to our destiny.

K.Wirtz Bodhisattva

Without emotions, darkness can not be turned into light and apathy is not in motion.

Carl Gustav Jung

The way to fulfill our destiny is usually dark for our consciousness. It is important not only to know the destiny but also the path that goes with it.

K.Wirtz Bodhisattva

I do not just want to appeal to your mind. I want to win your hearts.

Mahatma Gandhi

Not only body and mind, but also the soul wants to be nourished.

K.Wirtz Bodhisattva

From what you want to know and measure, you have to say goodbye, at least for a time. Only when you have left the city do you see how high their towers rise above the houses.

Friedrich Nietzsche

The farther I move worldly from you, the closer I come to your souls.

K.Wirtz Bodhisattva

It is the high destiny of man to serve more than to rule.

Albert Einstein

What is a human day, in the lifetime of a star?

K.Wirtz Bodhisattva

He who is truly benevolent can never be unhappy; who is really wise can never be confused; He who is truly brave never fears.

Confucius

The good is so close and often undiscovered. My way goes on, until the last recognizes.

K.Wirtz Bodhisattva

The true perfection of man is not in what he possesses, but what he is.

Oscar Wilde

Serene and patient, I often see the doggedness with which people cling to their habits, their usual habitual pain, not the clues to happiness to which they are repeatedly pushed.

K.Wirtz Bodhisattva

Without love, the rich are poor, the poor make them rich.

Aurelius Augustinus

It is not always easy to divert energies into useful paths when they come concentrated.

K.Wirtz Bodhisattva

You can not give the gift of love. It is waiting to be accepted.

Tagore

Do not expect the one to do it for you, which you are not ready to do for yourself.

K.Wirtz Bodhisattva

Love that loves from the heart is richest when it gives. Love that speaks of victims is not right love.

Emanuel Geibel

If we succeed in removing something from our thinking / consciousness, it will not exist for us, and if something unknown will be able to get into it, it will become real.

K.Wirtz Bodhisattva

The only important thing in life is the traces of love we leave when we have to leave and say goodbye.

Albert Schweitzer

Often the soul recognizes the charisma of another rather than our consciousness. That's why we feel attracted to someone before we can justify it.

K.Wirtz Bodhisattva

The man we loved is no longer where he was. But he is everywhere we are and commemorate him.

Aurelius Augustinus

People are like the poles of magnets, they attract or repel.

K.Wirtz Bodhisattva

You are not dead, you only exchanged the rooms, you live in me and go through my dreams.

Michelangelo

Let go of your thinking, your feelings, your desires, your fears, let them out and go and you will receive what makes you happy.

K.Wirtz Bodhisattva

In the course of time the soul takes on the color of the thoughts.

Marcus Aurelius

Born to suffer, suffer without being harmed, bear the burden of many to live in happiness.

K.Wirtz Bodhisattva

If you stretch a string to hard, it will break. If you make her weak, you can not play on her.

Buddha

Although no more true, but not lied, because the truth was, made room for a new truth.

K.Wirtz Bodhisattva

A ship should not be tied to a single anchor, and life should not be tied to a single hope.

Epictetus

Day names that are losing more and more importance for me, have to be painfully reminded when dealing with others.

Because time is meaningless for me.

K.Wirtz Bodhisattva

I have three treasures that I guard and cherish. One is love, the second is contentment, the third is humility. Only the lover is courageous, only the frugal is generous, only the humble is able to rule.

Lao Tzu

The rain is falling, the birds are chirping and both are not worried about what is and what they are and do.

K.Wirtz Bodhisattva

The desire for love is not the desire of love, but of vanity.

Friedrich Nietzsche

Live in love, humility and mindfulness, then "evil" will not surprise or harm you.

K.Wirtz Bodhisattva

Love is agony, lovelessness is death.

Marie von Ebner-Eschenbach

If there is love in you, there are also words of love, so there is also a smile of love, use it, before fear, envy and hate take away your love for a long time.

K.Wirtz Bodhisattva

Learning consists in remembering information that has lived in the soul of man for generations.

Socrates

When the feeling of love becomes so strong that it tears the ground from under the feet. To be dropped, to be carried by love.

K.Wirtz Bodhisattva

Dark are the ways that fate goes.

Euripidis

Souls are eternal, even stars pass away and are born again, because even stars are the same like souls or bodies.

K.Wirtz Bodhisattva

The stream of truth flows through channels of error.

Tagore

How should God punish love, act in the same way as the diabolical, or exactly the opposite with love, with role model?

K.Wirtz Bodhisattva

As one takes off worn clothes and puts on others, new ones, the soul also removes the worn-out bodies and enters into other, new ones.

Hindu proverb

Only those who can let go of thinking about disappointment will find peace. Peace is the requirement for true love.

K.Wirtz Bodhisattva

If God dwells in all that exists in the universe, if the scholar and the street sweeper are of God, then there is no one who is high, and none who are low, all are equal without limitation, they are equal because they are the same creatures of that creator are.

Mahatma Gandhi

The bond with the soulmate is so strong that joy and pain are felt over many thousands of miles.

K.Wirtz Bodhisattva

I am committed to the truth, as I recognize it every day, and not the permanence.

Mahatma Gandhi

Hearts always love, they call, cry (sometimes unconsciously for the mind) always to the soul mates, unless they have found him then they whisper caresses.

K.Wirtz Bodhisattva

If you want to get to know people, study their excuses.

William Faulkner

If you are a pure heart, fear nothing, adversities are the thorns of happiness and their poison the manna of the gods.

K.Wirtz Bodhisattva

We strive more to avoid pain than to gain joy.

Sigmund Freud

Nothing strange to me, nothing I do not understand and yet everything so hard, so easy.

K.Wirtz Bodhisattva

If we do not have peace, it is because we have forgotten that we belong together.

Mother Teresa

Every time I think that I'm tired of the sight of lovelessness / strife, the light of love shines in me and I am grateful.

K.Wirtz Bodhisattva

We do not need weapons and bombs to bring peace, we need love and compassion.

Mother Teresa

Look in the mirror, look deep into your eyes, hide everything else and see what happens.

K.Wirtz Bodhisattva

If everything seems to go against you, remember that the plane takes off against the wind, not with it.

Henry Ford

Is weeds of less value than a flower or the ugly duckling opposite the swan? Everything is made out of pure love.

K.Wirtz Bodhisattva

You have not lived today until you have done something for someone who can never pay you back.

John Bunyan

I am Buddhist, Christian, Muslim, Jew, Hindu, Tao, black, white, yellow, red, because I am love.

K.Wirtz Bodhisattva

Mildness is not a weakness. It takes courage to be good-natured in such a cruel world.

Beau Taplin

Having gained own insights, limited understanding, as great and true as they are at the moment, they are being replaced with expanded consciousness. They are therefore neither wrong nor right.

K.Wirtz Bodhisattva

Trade fast when it comes to correcting a mistake.

Confucius

From faith becomes knowledge and from knowledge it becomes an action, which one naturally does like breathing.

K.Wirtz Bodhisattva

The experience is like a lantern in the back; it always illuminates only the path we already have behind us.

Confucius

I am born, born again and again, again, as ... to love, to suffer, to comfort, to radiate until the last one overcomes his suffering.

K.Wirtz Bodhisattva

Friendship is a soul in two bodies.

Aristotle

Once all egotism is erased, there is no way back, even if the thinker in us tries to see it differently.

K.Wirtz Bodhisattva

Is not life given to us, so that we become richer in the mind, even if the external appearance has to suffer

Vincent van Gogh

Wars, catastrophes, illnesses scare the human body away, but the loving souls can not touch it.

K.Wirtz Bodhisattva

Do not close your eyes to suffering and do not let your consciousness dull for its existence.

Buddha

As long as there is a person who stands against hatred and violence with love, I am not afraid.

K.Wirtz Bodhisattva

There is a perfection deep in the midst of all inadequacy. There is a silence, deep in the midst of helplessness. There is a goal, deep in the midst of all worldly cares.

Buddha

As long as there are those who would gladly accept all the suffering of the world, I am not afraid.

K.Wirtz Bodhisattva

Knowledge should be replaced by wisdom, thereby worry will disappear. Wanting to grasp everything with the mind will drive wisdom away.

Asian wisdom

To love the suffering as well as the joy, the grief, the pain, the happiness, because love is without evaluation, in love all are the same.

K.Wirtz Bodhisattva

Not the best is the best, the best of all, but the one who overcomes himself.

Buddha

Bitterness sometimes appears as hardness and mostly it is only unprocessed disappointment. "Recognize"

K.Wirtz Bodhisattva

Everything created is transient. Strive on, make an effort to be constantly mindful.

Buddha

Only those who recognize themselves with absolute honesty will be able to change themselves positively.

K.Wirtz Bodhisattva

The evil that reviles the virtuous resembles the man who looks up and spits at the sky; his saliva does not pollute the sky, but falls down again and pollutes him.

Buddha

Everything is nothing and nothing is everything, but these words are also reviews that do not exist. One can not put into words for which there are no words. Words are only for the "little" human mind.

K.Wirtz Bodhisattva

Suffering ennobles man. Only those who endure suffering will be lucky.

Dalai Lama

A fatigue (not the physical) comes over us from deep inside, is the indication that the time to change is there.

K.Wirtz Bodhisattva

The deeper we see through suffering, the closer we come to the goal of liberation from suffering.

Dalai Lama

A heart is not open just because you think and say it is open. It will be broken until it is really completely open to the individual (s).

K.Wirtz Bodhisattva

If the desire for happiness was enough to bring it about, there would be no suffering, because no one seeks suffering.

Dalai Lama

If you recognize how you are and you do not like it, do not look for excuses why you are so, seek to change yourself.

K.Wirtz Bodhisattva

The real essence of the mind is light; Darkening may only be temporary.

Dalai Lama

Give, it will be given to you. Hold on, it will be taken.

K.Wirtz Bodhisattva

I have to fight the pain of others, because it is just as painful as my own. The others are sentient beings just like me. That's why I have to act for her sake.

Dalai Lama

If everyone in friendship, love, or humanity, would be able to help a poorer, weaker one without expectation, there would be no poverty or war.

K.Wirtz Bodhisattva

First of all, you should consider carefully how similar one is to the other: you experience joy and sorrow just like me. That's why I have to protect her like myself.

Dalai Lama

Also in the discipline you should not forget the joy, because without joy it becomes a torment.

K.Wirtz Bodhisattva

If you argue with dear friends, refer only to the current situation - let the past rest.

Dalai Lama

From time to time you should take a candle for every concern, label it with your worries, light it in the dark and watch as the worries burns.

K.Wirtz Bodhisattva

Share your knowledge, so you gain immortality.

Dalai Lama

He who does not believe in himself will not believe in life. What you think becomes your reality.

K.Wirtz Bodhisattva

Remember, the best relationship is one in which love for another is greater than desire for another.

Dalai Lama

Individual days and their names are losing more and more importance in my reality.

K.Wirtz Bodhisattva

Ideas like my nation, your nation, my religion, your religion have become secondary. On the contrary, we must emphasize that the other is worth as much as we ourselves. That is humanity! That's why we need to rethink our whole education system.

Dalai Lama

Thoughts and feelings are like the wind, sometimes a gentle breeze and sometimes like a hurricane thoughts and feelings are like the fire, often warming and sometimes burning, thoughts and feelings are like the water, flowing in the smallest cracks, like the surf and as sweeping as rapids, thoughts and feelings are also like the earth, the soil on which everything can grow, but also how the desert withers

Thoughts and feelings are elements, are dimension, are love, are everything.

K.Wirtz Bodhisattva

Everyone has good qualities - you just have to be willing to find them. When you do that, then you have to admit that your negative view of a person is based on their own perception, more on their mental projection than on the true nature of that person.

Dalai Lama

You do not have to close old doors when you're ready to go through new ones. Old doors will dissolve and become unreachable for you.

K.Wirtz Bodhisattva

The irony wants it so that when we have the object of our desires, we are still not satisfied. In this way, desire never ends and is a constant source of trouble. The only antidote is the contentment.

Dalai Lama

People are like the poles of magnets, they attract or repel each other.

K.Wirtz Bodhisattva

I feel that a person whose actions are designed to make others happy, certainly experiences less unhappiness in life than someone who does not. Sickness, old age, mishaps and the like hit us all the same. But the suffering that undermines our inner peace - worry, doubt, failure - is definitely less.

Dalai Lama

Divine love is the food for our salvation.

K.Wirtz Bodhisattva

The misfortune that is happening to us today is the karmic, cause and effect, retribution of injustice we have done to others. Our own negative actions in the past create the conditions for our present suffering. If we think it right, we are actually the one who harms another: whoever harms us accumulates negative karma for us, laying the foundation for his future suffering.

Dalai Lama

Through dark valleys, over icy peaks, I wandered to realize that true happiness is in me in another dimension.

K.Wirtz Bodhisattva

A person who thinks more about the others is much more balanced, calmer, and happier than people who always think only of themselves.

Dalai Lama

If you live in true love, even water will taste sweet as honey.

K.Wirtz Bodhisattva

Can we hate someone who is a slave to his own disturbing emotions, harming others and eventually destroying himself? Does not he rather deserve our sympathy?

Dalai Lama

If you live beyond ratings, nothing will destroy you. You will not feel pain or illness. You are just love.

K.Wirtz Bodhisattva

As you deepen your spiritual practice and focus on compassion and wisdom, you will repeatedly encounter the suffering of other sentient beings. And you develop the ability to perceive it, to respond to it and to feel deep compassion instead of apathy or fainting.

Dalai Lama

There is no big or small, no hard or easy, because everything "IS" big, small, light or heavy, are just reviews in our thinking.

K.Wirtz Bodhisattva

If you have to be selfish - that's my advice - be wise selfish. Wise people serve others sincerely and put others' needs above their own. In the end, you will be happier. The kind of egoism that causes struggles, killing, theft, harsh words, or neglecting the well-being of others - will result in your own loss.

Dalai Lama

Better a stony path of love than a path of greed filled with diamonds.

K.Wirtz Bodhisattva

The development of inner values is similar to physical activity. The more we train our skills, the stronger we become. The difference is that unlike the body, there is no limit to how much we can go in the development of the mind.

Dalai Lama

When you do your best (at the moment) it is never wrong. Wrong are only the reviews of others, which is not enough.

K.Wirtz Bodhisattva

What are you searching for? After luck, love, peace of mind? Do not look for it at the other end of the world, otherwise you will return disappointed, bitter and desperate. Search on the other end of yourself afterwards, in the depths of the heart.

Tibetan wisdom

If something is not going to be closed all doors there, you realize what should be open the most unlikely ways.

K.Wirtz Bodhisattva

Farewell and death are just other words for a new beginning and life. Everything you leave behind can be found in a different form again and again.

Tibetan wisdom

Behind promises, with all their strength and love, even if contrary to newly learned and knowledge, they stand above their own destiny, it causes suffering when one tries to evaluate it.

K.Wirtz Bodhisattva

You are not on earth to be unhappy. But happiness is only the inner peace. Learn to find him. You can do it. Overcome yourself and you will overcome the world.

Buddhist wisdom

Because of past experiences, we should not forget what the future holds for us.

K.Wirtz Bodhisattva

They argue with each other and contradict each other only the people who only see part of the whole truth.

Buddhist wisdom

Anyone who acts against his purpose, regardless of the reasons, will suffer until he has recognized the way.

K.Wirtz Bodhisattva

Everything depends on the way of thinking. Everything starts with thinking, everything is directed and created. Those who speak or act badly are followed by suffering like the wheel of the hoofs of the draft animal.

Buddhist wisdom

One should not contradict one's own natural needs by waiting for one's soulmate (usually one does not know who it is) enjoy the beautiful hours as long as they last, do not suffer when they are over, because with the soulmate the hours of sunshine will be infinite.

K.Wirtz Bodhisattva

Just be careful! Allow all things to take their proper or natural course. Then your mind becomes quieter and quieter, wherever you are. He becomes as quiet as a clear forest pond. Then all sorts of great and rare animals will approach this pond to drink from it. So you will learn to understand the nature of all things in the world. So you will see many wonderful, strange things come and go. But you will stay quiet. Problems will arise. But you will see through it. This is the happiness of an awakened person.

Buddhist wisdom

Expectations are nothing other than your own "not recognizing" the truthfulness.

K.Wirtz Bodhisattva

Among us who are locked up in the dark and narrow cage that we have built ourselves and whom we believe to be the universe as a whole, there are few who can even imagine that there is another dimension of reality ,

Sogyal Rinpoche

I let go of all dependencies, so what should I fear?

K.Wirtz Bodhisattva

There are only two days a year that you can not do anything. One is yesterday, the other tomorrow. This means that today is the right day to love, faith and, first and foremost, to live.

Dalai Lama

Praise, whether from others or from oneself, is important to human, encouraging one's own actions, when one is doing (and only occasionally) in oneself and one's doubts or causes doubts caused by others.

K.Wirtz Bodhisattva

The first disadvantage of anger is that it destroys their inner peace. The second is that your view of reality is distorted. When you think about it, you will understand that anger do not help us, but only have a destructive effect on us. Thus, we can begin to distance ourselves from anger when these feelings arise in us.

Dalai Lama

Not the people you do not expect hurt you, but the expectations you place on these people.

K.Wirtz Bodhisattva

The exercise in patience saves us from losing our serenity. This gives us the opportunity to train our judgment, even in very difficult situations. It gives us inner space. And through this space, we gain a degree of self-restraint that allows us to respond appropriately to situations. Compassionate rather than driven by our anger and annoyance.

Dalai Lama

Feelings are beyond languages and they do not need them.

K.Wirtz Bodhisattva

He who seeks the truth must not be afraid when he finds it.

Asian wisdom

If you are in a certain state of consciousness, it is quite possible to be constantly in meditation while doing other mundane worldly things.

K.Wirtz Bodhisattva

Plan the difficult thing where it is still easy! Do the big thing where it is still small! All gravity on earth always begins as easy. Everything great on earth, always starts as a small one.

Asian wisdom

Life is changeable as the weather, sometimes the wind comes from the front, sometimes in the back, rain or sunshine. Stay calm and calm like a deep-rooted tree.

K.Wirtz Bodhisattva

What is in tune resonates with each other. What is related in the innermost essence, that seeks each other

Asian wisdom

Everything we do in love serves peace, everything we do in peace also serves love.

K.Wirtz Bodhisattva

The author and why Bodhisattva

My last birth took place in September 1959. Although I had a normal and loving childhood, I was always confronted with suffering at a young age. My second oldest brother, a premature baby and blind. In addition, epileptics. My oldest brother who got into the drug scene. My mother, who died of liver cirrhosis in my arms at the age of 60. The death of my father, of which I learned only years later. Just to name a few things. But my later life as adolescent and as an adult were constantly marked by unrest, strife, rebellion and struggle.

Nevertheless, I came again and again with people who sought comfort, encouragement and help with me. Strangely enough, I also almost always had some advice or solution to their problems. Only my own was not under my control. Of course I did not understand it then. Anyway, I eventually got to the point where I no longer wanted and was ready to put an end to my life, when suddenly everything changed. I met my soul mate and Yasodhara. I first came in contact with real love. The previous relationships were more likely to be in love.

Nevertheless, I was still faced with suffering and strife, but I was better able to accept this and deal with it. My fate then took me to the deportation camp in Sri Lanka. All ways to escape from this camp closed for me.

There I made my first conscious meditation experiences. Another campinasse not only explained many things to me, but also gave me important clues for my spiritual advancement. At this point a big thank you for him.

I soon had my first experiences with "light". A light that could not be of this world. My Buddhist teacher spoke of "enlightenment" Development did not stop. Once, in deep meditation, I managed to talk to a mosquito about its purpose. I learned to deepen my skills, especially those of healing, even over long distances. Sometimes I managed to heal people and sometimes not. I also did not understand its meaning. Strangers came to me and wanted to be blessed. (I had no idea why and felt strange accordingly). Next, "light experiences, enlightenments" followed as well as understanding and knowing about things and their context.

At some point, even my "teacher" wondered how far and how fast the development progressed. My teacher then left the camp.

Peace was growing around me and within me, and even the greatest troublemakers changed their behavior in my area.

Apparently I had learned enough in the camp and it opened a way to leave the camp.

Again I was led to people in need whom I could help. This was followed by another milestone in my development. I was on the way to do errands daily when I suddenly noticed how my "soul" was divided. She beamed over me and then fanned in different directions, held by invisible bands that converged in me. One direction was flying birds with which I could talk in flight, as well as being in trees and stones at the same time, listening and understanding a conversation that was conducted thousands of miles away in a language unknown to me. Nevertheless, I did not lose the mindfulness for the traffic on which my body still took part.

There were still many insights, in an almost frightening speed. I just had to look at things or think about them and understand everything about them.

Then the question or the fork in the road appears in me, which path I should take. The way to Nirvana, in eternal enlightenment in true love and deep rest, or that of a Bodhisattva who is reborn again and again until the last sorrow is extinguished.

For a long time I tested this question in myself and suddenly the answer was there without me having to give it. That's when I realized that "light" can smile.

I am learned the conversation with the light. I ask questions on the spiritual level or give answers without me thinking this and the "light" counters me with different luminosities.

As out-of-body soul journeys have become normal to me, I am currently engaged in overcoming physical laws and altering diseased cells and genes in the body

Many in the human world may think I'm a nutcase, I understand that too, but the knowledge in me leaves me with a mild smile.

Epilogue

I hope not only that you liked this book, but that you can take advantage of it.

That your life changes and enriches in the way you wish it to be.

If you have any questions, please feel free to contact the e-mail address given in the imprint. I will answer as soon as possible and seriously.

May my knowledge, my power and my energy be with you on all your journey to peace and love.

"So be it"

Thank you

www.ingramcontent.com/pod-product-compliance
Ingram Content Group UK Ltd.
Pitfield, Milton Keynes, MK11 3LW, UK
UKHW020126250726
13967UKWH00002B/510